I0079063

Shearsman

double issue

83 & 84

**Summer
2010**

Edited by
Tony Frazer

Shearsman magazine is published in the United Kingdom by
Shearsman Books Ltd
58 Velwell Road
Exeter EX4 4LD

www. shearsman.com

ISBN 978-1-84861-109-2
ISSN 0260-8049

Acknowledgements:

One of the poems by Swantje Lichtenstein appeared in German in the volume
Landen (Lyrikedition 2000, Munich, 2009), copyright © Lyrikedition 2000. The
poems by Gertrud Kolmar are taken from *Welten* (Suhrkamp Verlag, Frankfurt-
am-Main, 1947), copyright © Suhrkamp Verlag, 1999; thanks to Suhrkamp
Verlag for permission to print these translations. The translations of poems
by Jorge Palma are printed here by permission of the author. Stephen Watts'
translation of Ziba Karbassi's 'Collage Poem 10' has already appeared in the
author's chapbook *Collage Poems* (Exiled Writers Ink, 2009)

Subscriptions and single copies:

Back issues from n° 63 onwards (uniform with this issue)—cost £8.50/$13.50
through trade channels. Single copies can be ordered for £8.50, post-free, direct
from the press, or from bookstores in the UK and the USA. Earlier issues, from
1 to 62, may be had for £3 each direct from the press, but contact us for prices
for a full, or partial, run. Current subscriptions—covering two double-issues,
each around 108 pages, cost £13 in the UK, £16 for the rest of Europe (incl.
Republic of Ireland), and £18 for the rest of the world Longer subscriptions
may be had for a proportionately higher payment, which insulates purchasers
from further price-rises during the term of the subscription.

Submissions

Shearsman operates a submissions-window system, whereby submissions are
only considered during the months of March and September, at which point
selections are made for the October and April issues respectively. Submissions
may be sent by mail or email, but email attachments—other than PDFs—are
not accepted. We aim to respond within 2–3 months of the window's closure.

CONTENTS

The Dream-Clock

Daytrip on the Enterprise

Dublin
D 09.35 D
U 09.35 U
B 09.35 B
L 09.35 L
I 09.35 I
N 09.35 N

Belfast
B 18.10 B
E 18.10 E
L 18.10 L
F 18.10 F
A 18.10 A
S 18.10 S
T 18.10 T

Dep
Drogheda
D 10.06 D
R 10.06 R
O 10.06 O
G 10.06 G

Dep
Drogheda
D 19.41 D
R 19.41 R
O 19.41 O
G 19.41 G

```
B O Y N E   V   I A D U C T   B   O Y N E V   I   A D U C T
O Y N E   V I   A D U C T   B O   Y N E V   I A   D U C T
Y N E   V I A   D U C T   B O Y   N E V   I A D   U C T
N E   V I A D   U C T   B O Y N   E V   I A D U   C T
E   V I A D L   C T   B O Y N E   V   I A D U C   T
N E   V I A D   U C T   B O Y N   E V   I A D U   C T
Y N E   V I A   D U C T   B O Y   N E V   I A D   U C T
O Y N E   V I   A D U C T   B O   Y N E V   I A   D U C T
B O Y N E   V   I A D U C T   B   O Y N E V   I   A D U C T
```

H 10.06 H
E 10.06 E
D 10.06 D
A 10.06 A
Arr
Belfast
B 11.45 B
E 1.45 E
L 11.45 L
F 11.45 F
A 11.45 A
S 11.45 S
T 11.45 T

H 19.41 H
E 19.41 E
D 19.41 D
A 19.41 A
Arr
Dublin
D 20.20 D
U 20.20 U
B 20.20 B
L 20.20 L
I 20.20 I
N 20.20 N

from Essays in island logic

> 'Same sea, same dangers waiting for him
> As though he had got nowhere but older'
> W.S. Merwin —'Odysseus'

he considers the passage of time

old man walking retirement

up the hillside below the pine belts
past centuries-old spilled

sarcophagi looking
to recover one particular grave *stele*—
this

sure as he can be
this one under a triangular pediment
the young man leaning back in bas relief

such a contemporary slouch
legs crossed at the ankles hips thrust out
in contemplation

a warrior's helmet held at arm's length
its long plume

like a lion's tail
seeming about to respond to his ambitious

nature his searching
out the end of all complexity—

sees now the boy's had his forehead
chipped off
the kid is brainless and beautiful

about second century BC
marking the grave of a dead warrior

an old man all but forgotten
after dusk

walking retirement down the dark hillside
bringing it to the surf's edge now

like a child

he has to make his own bed

loves this steady climb
even to find she's stripped it to launder

has to pull clean from the creaking basket
launch sheets across it
fisting pillows into pillowcase mouths

all the time believing he should
but tonight finding it
difficult to resist the siren past—

men of the island
who built bedrooms about olive trees

gnarled trunks trimmed until smooth
an adze steady in hand

only pausing to run a finger
up the solid bed-post then falling to
eager and passionate

pushing on to confirm
the firm centre

the writhe and rhythm of generation—

absurd and primitive
as deep purple dye inlaid with silver
and gold

yet each achieved a royal bed of sorts
roots at their furthest reaches

growing intimate with roots of neighbours'
straining olives he feels now

too queasy a thought
one hand heavy on the banister's climb

to uneventful bed

his son wakes and wanders round the house

stirring in the small of night

the boy raises himself to a gluey throat
fattened lips

feels his way
downstairs to the unlit kitchen

to be surprised by the winking of lights
like campfire signs
wasteful stand-bys burning

on the distant hillside
of radio microwave fridge oven—

leans into polished taps
knocks back glass after re-hydrating glass

dregs of last night's beer
incline him to hear the muttering of troops

on the dark flanks of hills

the clank of billies scouring of blade edges
a vastness of purpose
drawing up the life he never possessed—

knows he would have been astute
clear-headed then
consulted through the terrific nights

by faithful generals
who'd hymn his black ferocity

his desire for the acid tests of dawn
that will never come
but the obscurities of blame

upstairs his father singing in his sheets
dull as new-born

his wife is restless in her sleep

a girl once more shepherding the flock
of twenty geese

like pets she lords it over them
a pack of baying dogs

showing pale against dark volcanic soil
waddling from the round pond

on her father's farm
crowding to eat the grain she lends them

till eagle cruelty with steely talons
sweeps out of a sky apparently twenty
years deep—

feathers
explosive as when white cherry blossom
is ripped by the wind

a blur of wing white/black failing

she screams wrestling to beat
the bird off in vain
her flock a shredded bloodied mattress —

imperious eagle on the roof-tree

tilting its eye to ocean distance
into blue ocean
it's me your husband come to set you free

her sphere of influence diminished
twenty-fold

but continues to be grateful
touching heaviness in her right breast
cannot recall

how many times she has dreamed this

his son's dream is a new beginning

it blows like Mount St Helens

some plantation farmer
offering three women he knows
as unwilling sacrifice

to appease what he seriously calls
the volcanic gods—

but the DJ declines

there are too few people laughing
too many climbing into the front of trucks

all lights and reasonable instruments
melted in the first blast

all wax-hanging globules of plastic
a new native art

ripening towards exploitation
as individuals begin to paint
volcanic ash in albumen

as if that mix might
usher in secure economic government
a bright-lit future—

others regardless are beginning
to reconfigure Year Zero
till no-one confesses suffering troubled

sleep sense of impotence
strange unfixable guilts resistant

even to waking
as if what just hurtled with such clarity
through a young man's head

might never happen

Poem, including history

'Cad a dhéanfaimid feasta gan adhmad?'

When we drove to Kilcash a lorry-
load of timber hove out of a dip
as we pulled in; it must have been
on its way down from the Coillte
plantation above, though the sign
read CUL DE SAC. We'd been on about
Caoilte's elegy for the Fianna
the castle wore a scaffold-shroud
and a mock-Alpine stockbroker folly
had sprouted against Sliabh na mBan.

Down in the chapel-shell
Philip Ryan (unkindly and in defiance
of likelihood I think him
one of the Helper ilk, whose cog was got
for the malice that gave Cromwell
ale or a secret pass—I forget what
just as they are not forgotten) has lain
ten times longer than he lived
beneath the clutter of *arma Christi*,
an egg timer and an energetic Crucifixion
which might just as easily have been
executed in the days of Muireadach
Albanach Ó Dálaigh as at the date
of the chaste inscription.

Back then, stasis put people on the road
and they looked for respite in the close
dark of a quatrain. They slept like strangers
in a grimy kip, loosening holsters
and scabbards, keeping favoured hands free,
facing the door. In the middle of the night
because it was precisely what they had
done all through their history
they turned round, and fought.

Poem, occluding history

That ruin on the green
clipped by ivy, overleant by sallies
isn't the monastic site
it's a handball alley.

That board tells visitors
in some crabbed dialect
of Official where they stood
when Froissart was got.

That hair!—that accent!
No wonder people send
you the long road round
and your fly down—clearly a Prod.

That low block kirk's
where Dermody lilted
hardly a stone in the close
not moss-blasted, obliterated.

That gully is the Seven Holy Wells
scarcely less calculated to spook
the daytripper than a grove
sacred to Crom Cruach.

That dizened tree. Rosaries,
photographs, statuettes,
inhalers, bootees. St Senchall's
fame was the cure of cataracts.

That cold gust means rain. The tokens
whirl about, neither emblems
nor effects of supplicants who
aren't quite dupes, nor yet heathens.

Killeigh, 2009

Unlike ourselves

'ungelic is us . . .'

Here, warden, wake up!
our cur's to the greenwood gone
and all our sweet silly songs

blasted.

angler—
    wrecker—
        wanker—

     wræce.

Here in this bigriver hundred
this blackwater parish
departed glamour left us

gutted.

Eely—
    seely—
       yellowbelly—

     hwelp.

Here's to the last-stand merchants
the king over the gashy fen
only a gift to the poets

shafted.

sissy—
    sot—
      sap—

    scop.

Here I am on this scrogg; they're quartered
on that. If they only knew what
I'm thinking they'd have me

sectioned.

Relinquish song

> hop light on dirty feet
> creep close sole light
> down in along the strait
> breach blaze the vault
> glib honey light
> foot by foot

We renounce
our tongue for day reseal parole
nonce words in their peculiar order.

We retreat
from range to settlement
nomadism to quest
(and back again)
from seely fear of fell beasts
to staple starch and dental caries.

We repudiate
our wan daughters
                such bloody engagement
pain certainty abandoned for seed lore
except where it recurs pure
as her—spindly—and her cross mommet.

(We reproach
your speculation on this matter.)

We recant
our aniconic religion
for gods like men only bigger
except in effigy
when they are smaller
though not always
(often the face
of the diminutive being
displays a somewhat
dolorous expression).
We laughed when you showed us
your figurines too late
to remark you were not laughing.

We repeal
empirical reasoning
for swaddy bloody feet
pharaohs' elbows

> spring or fall
> equinox
> on the plain
> upland cut
> the thread that
> stitches earth
> to sky in
> six taut cords
> then chop each
> reed string in
> sixty-one
> erect your struts
> catch your bright
> particular
> star between
> swing your load
> three six six
> ticks
> > tsk

We reject
that rule quick
as the dread ash lych stick.

We revoke
exogamy, totemism, public coition, cannibalism
tattooing and the participation of women in battle.

(You too, hn?)

We refuse
nothing and no-one:
a silver cauldron
a sunbright bull
a tank intercom
rigged to burn
motherfucker burn
aren't they all the one?

We refute
proportion
making the earth our comfit
ourselves mites on a mote.

We repress
the intimate kind code:
would anyone kill his father
if he were able to help it?
A girl weaves her ribs
with her matron-murderer's
no comfort for them
for us comfort.

We retire
when you feel us pressing
on the walls of your world
you do not know what has touched you
                              and

We recede
down away along the shaft to bide.

You are dazzled by our quartz piazza.

Undersong

> *I am storing fifty-one seeds of Goatsbeard:*
> *so I can sow again.*
> *Now I have lost them. Now I search again.*
> Bill Griffiths

Bill, I was all set to write something
for the children who worked down the mine:
the trappers on the tram-ways & the barrow-ways;

the bairns who kept their heads down
and for their pains
were made shovers & skeekers,

hewers & headsmen,
landing-lads & foal-putters;
the ones who, when their lives could not be carried in the common
        tongue,

invented speech to fit: North's undersong,
a dialect within a dialect, the kind of thing
(you'd have said) poets like to take the credit for.

Bill, I was all set to send that email
when I heard you'd died—
so I picked up your last book (*Pitmatic: the Talk of the North East Coalfield*)

where, quoted in Parliamentary Papers
from 1842 (Volume 16:
Commissioners' Reports on working practice down the mine),

I found this from a boy—an unnamed Seaham boy—
who went down at the age of eight:
I had six candles from my father.

I liked it very well at first
but then I had an accident.
The tub broke my arm in two places.

I had a coal fall on my forehead
and the mark remains, and will always remain.
I got no smart money.

The Mystery of Glass

My sister has gone outside now.
I do not know if she feels the rain,
sees ragged crow dragging his
frayed feet above the field,
smells clover mead reigned
over by brown kye, crown-
uddered as queens.

Perhaps she walks the clouded hill
with me, watches the firth evaporate,
the crags disintegrate,
the undulating land whisper
its muted antiphon from crypt
to misted crypt crouching
between cached sunshine—

caught between
yes and yes,
a russet hind
hugging tarnished
gorse edge—

maybe she stops to thrust her thumb
into the foxglove maw,
eager to silence that mauve throat
for now or evermore,
its prescience, its deadly
digitalis roar, or runs ahead
to meet the many-faced magenta stare
of rose-bay willow-herb stabbing
honeysuckle-crept floor
where mitred *felix mas*
waves tawny-haired
munificence, broadcasting
dusky spoor where thrush

scatters her ashy unsung song,
soothsaying robin
and slight wren run;

or waits beside harebell-rung
verge where dreamy dissemblies
spin of thistle's burnt-out stars
to watch the swallows harvesting
their dancing wheat-flung
fare in leaping pas de chat,
unearthly, sown in air—

wing

as she
sliding
severing
light diving
dividing
shuddering stalk
from flower a-gawp,
lisping
its scented song
of where
colours
come from

or leaf
in bright diatribe
against the wind's
wild cry
of coming rain,
beside itself
with life

in love
with clandestine

flow of time
hunting oblivion
for fragments
of itself

rain

kissing the street, the
earth, the unforgiving stain,
veil of heaven-sent
remorse, or grief,
missing seen
crystal through
crystal to
crystal bead
upon the ground

a bird
a memory of flight
or origin of height
higher than soprano
shift of tongue, a
touch alit upon
by notes and shine,

into the citrus throat
of toadflax slides
a drop of sky,
parched calyx swallows
wept rebirth
preserving it
until some quaking sun
in passing snaps
and slakes its thirst—

giving and taking
is all we know—

tell me a teardrop
from its wild cousin,
tell me the truth.

(I waited
and you did not come.
Outside a bird
sang my obliteration,
rain fell unendingly
it seemed; night
came and went
and day reconvened

again)

and again I was excluded. Entrances
and exits were made, instructions issued
and laws obeyed; I saw the endless carnival
repeat itself and all of life was spectacle.
Here is the meaning: truth
does not come round again
but is the very constant sustenance.
Do we describe the peril that we do not know
but by hunger and enforced abstinence?

Breaking the bond with fear
is agony. All is still in here.
The clock enunciates its
mannered order, as pre-planned,
as if shared dream
was waking certainty;
the potent march of minutes manned

against contingency. A web
of terror holds in place
the chair, the wall,

the lacquered carapace.
A scream defies the law
whereby each atom may flee
in sudden preference for east,

yet each door opens
upon a furnished void
declaiming its deficiency;
a silent plea for warmth,
occupancy to interrupt
the rage spanning each mute
relationship from ledge to pane.

pain

Today she is tired,
fatigued, she says,
and in the mirror
above the mantelpiece
watches the parade,
the busy business of the street:
devoid of destination, delayed,
foiled by a double act of light
obedient to her need for
more time. The day

is weeping. She waits,
kept in abeyance
by the steepness of the stair,
the self-absorption
of the cat, the sapphire
surface of a tile, square sunlight
listing jasmine. Her
husband is not there.

She waited. Rain
crept down

the window pane
as wept
across porcelain
cheek of denied
Madonna,
led by light,
sky white
holding
her son
oh
lacryma
sistere.

then

Back then, great-grandfather
built his world of glass
(thirteen children
and every one survived) a
shard for every living joy
('the higher up the mountain,
the greener grows the grass')
recalcitrant boy sent
upstairs to his room
('the more a donkey wags his tail
the more he shows his . . .')
the maid reports to master.

Heart pierced, he knew
(the higher up the mountain)
what his lad saw through.
It was his vocation.
The wonder of it, not
solid nor quite a-flow, the
wealth of it (a bell-pull in
every room), slow
vitrification, great

heat, the memory of sea,
stealthy, manifold solitudes
coalescing yet
not admitting night,
keeping faith with some
forgotten law
transmitted by the tide.

Looking up, he saw
where it all began:
a glittering cascade, a
shuddering, dissembling
span of spectra shattered
in song not of some
wayward child but
belonging to everyone.

face

I was his granddaughter's
darling, her coveted one,
the one she saw in the mirror
each time of day,
each way she looked at me
I was descended from her truth,
the loved, the pirouetting lie
they told. I saw it too.
I was the one
who looked away

to face

and now I am on the street
shuffling like time along
its grey meridian,
my sister somewhere near,

and she whose womb we knew
in great old age lets go
a sudden flood of blood
as if reliving maidenhood,
and then grows young again,
regains vitality, and neither
nurse nor doctor can divine
disease or calculate a cause—

it was her memory,
tripped by the spotted
wally-dog upon her windowsill,
the faded wooden babushka
monitoring her decline from atop
the tv set, the bed that cantilevers
up and down. Trapped
daughters in her lap,
hiding behind her apron,
trying on her headscarf
in the dark, tap,
tapping to come out.

At last we spoke.
'The atmosphere,' she said,
'of one's mind changes.'
I said, 'Don't look at
what I wear.' She said,
'Do I recall correctly
that your son has pale hair?'
I said, 'You should
have been there.'

She turned her head.
'The tree,' she said.

After everyone has gone
she sits on in the space
they leave behind, draped

in another century, struggling
to understand how the same
death has stolen in upon
her twice, and under
the same name.

Sitting at the table
studying the medical
dictionary: stepfather
and now daughter—
what sickness levels
generations without shame?

A frozen fall of light. She wonders
if she should go outside,
if she would recognise
the people that she met,
her kin, the chosen,
the assimilated friend.

She told me once
how time eschewed
the crude perambulations
of the clock, enfolding
each and every age,
sometimes in tenderness,
sometimes in rage;
revealing incidence
where second sight breaks
through (seventh child
of a seventh child). Her
first daughter answers
to her name.

We come and go.
We see what we are shown,
we know what we may know.

now

Long gone the hutted
bodger who turned
and tamed the beech-wood
stave; pale anemone
adrift between his feet,
pignut asleep in
pennoned loamy grave—

above, a cold white weight
hurled at black bark,
the sharp-edged scent
of arboreal blood;
awful pallor upturned
and glistening, as fallen
as a stillborn moon
expressing tears—
too soon, too soon—
between circlets
of hurried youth.

A thousand deaths ascend,
are clasped and carried
to the sea by she
who comprehends
the womb: never
too many, never
too few.

At last set free from light and lead
I watch the stained-glass saints
approach along the orchard path,
running to meet me in the copse
where God made Granny's bentwood chair;
dark-eyed, shedding rainbows they come
with apple-blossom in their hair,
and each one bare-heeled in the grass
where swerving adder lets her pass.

4 May 2009

Towns in the great desert (1)

The frozen river zigzags through the many-layered city.
The bars all empty on snow
while stranded cars sleep moored to old boats
rusted into landmarks.
She wakes from a dream of pounding doors,
her head racing like a wired alarm clock.
She walks through the house, naming the chairs
while a neighbour's cat
purrs in imagined kinship.
If you climb down into the snow,
a bird on a windowsill says,
you will find the sun is waiting there too.

A fine wind blows over the ice.
At a corner where
two streets are facing the end of explanations,
she watches a small boy squat to collect ants.
Just now he's noticed how in this place
the shells of ants
are crackling with inner fire.

Night serves a writ against travellers.
A woman arrives with two children asleep in a matchbox.
She unwraps the linen that binds their limbs
and places them side by side
on the mantelpiece.
Soon a small tree
is curving the memory of forests
over their unwritten faces.

Towns in the great desert (2)

The size of tall-masted ships,
of a spire of prayer,

the gate of hammered earth
and nailed wooden planks
is wheeled shut at second watch.
Guards wield huge feral dogs on iron chains
while other dogs laze about unchained
to supervise late arrivals.

The last to make his way through the closing gates,
he drags himself with the stumps of his arms,
battered legs trailing over stony ground.
Each night he sleeps in an old car,
turns the motor to a slow hum, climbs
into the engine, curls up beside its warmth,
locks the bonnet behind him.
His skin at dawn has the black fragrance of oil.
Each day he stretches out on the beach
to be pounded clean by the surf.
His body has the purple glow
of finely tuned mallets.

In the sky of this town there are no passing clouds or stars,
only the unbroken wall of millennial dust.
Sea water is all there is
to cook, to bathe, to wash.
To buy water to drink
they send their children to slave in distant mines.
Of this town they say
"The gods never came here."

Towns in the great desert (3)

Arrived here from the outside
you stop in wonder:
lights swaying in tall
honeycombs of glass.
Against the starless sky

seen across the flat dark water
these shells of lives lit up from the inside
exposed at random, so close, almost touchable.

Behind the transparency of glass
the lights spell something you cannot name
as if a summons from somewhere inside yourself
you have never travelled to,
as if here you could begin again.
Snow falls into your hands.
You stand watching in a small square
where a golden tree goes on defying winter.
A woman on a caged balcony
releases a dove into the frozen desert wind.
In a cubicle made of light
two men unpack a box
filled with stones.

Towns in the great desert (4)

They have built their parallel town
on the plateau of the clouds.
The intersecting patchwork of ladders
has at last found firm foundation.
Meticulously
they have dragged everything with them—
tarpaulins, cardboard boxes, tin sheets, old car-frames—
to establish the first favela of the clouds.
They have rigged up their TV sets
to the random migrations of lightning.
Lounging back in deckchairs like elegant movie stars
they sip all day through long straws
on a fine distillation of water vapour.
Meanwhile, stung by a sudden jealousy, the rich
go by in planes that look like oversized tourist buses.

Most of all
to this undulating plateau of spun clouds
they have brought their dead in wooden boxes.
What could never find place on earth
is safely at home here.
When the desert dwellers below
think the sky is groaning under the heavy weight of cloudbanks
it's no trick of the wind, no clinking in the wheels
of the enormous sky factory
that reprocesses salt.

Peacefully far above us
the dead are snoring.

Towns in the great desert (5)

What mattered most in the dream
was the quality of blue in the water
so that it wasn't about the naked young man, my rival,
doing handstands and backflips into the canal
or any wince of pain from contemplating in reverse image
the hammered remnants of my own body.
Like the perfect alignment of sailboats on a blue sea,
between the world and the world
the canal made a corridor
for whales and the white refuse of icebergs
to drift between familiar department stores,
the takeaway, the news-stand and the corner pub.
Suddenly how far away from death I was
standing alone and speechless
before the waters of the sky,
this proof
that the depths go on shining.

James Berger

Two Sonnets from *Transmit or Transmiss*

Coiled there to a summit in absolute separation,
laughing and brainless and scolding me,
seated, covered with branches, wriggling,
like an artery to the heart,
dug in, entrenched, implacable.
I'd just swum up, just awakened,
and now we meet in this awkward way,
I mean, with no pants and my penis pointing
like an index craving a definition.
Part statue, part liquid, part reverberation,
she circles around me seven times.
Each time I sink lower and feel a different wind
in my testicles, until she's flattened on top of me, wearing a new face.
The word for mirror echoes the word for hope.

The word for word rhymes with the word for bird.
Winged ruins hiccup into odysseys.
Nefertiti's head fits onto headless Venus
and I'm the suitor fucking my inner Penelope,
saying, yes yes, shove your husband's
arrow up my ass, and let me arrive,
let me return. Long years with stuffed ears
to reach this point.
The triangle is the shape for contemplation.
A vast catalogue of heads and bodies,
each in various ways identically beautiful.
I'm always at two points, in love with the third.
I'm always opening the door to my house,
then killing every inhabitant but one.

Mercury Heart

Poetry is the past that breaks out in our hearts.
                    Rainer Maria Rilke

For Henry Wellcome

Mind, it's merely a muscle laced with mercury
its human glow shrunk to fit a crystal case

there the heart is labelled with lucid letters
'Human', says the fading caption 'aged four'.

Maybe the child died in a dingy workhouse
then was butchered after a fatal bout of fever

to end up as a quaint keepsake on display,
some dead physician's claim to undying fame.

Quicksilver spread like a cold net in the vanes
but purged the meat of a child's brief poetry.

Quietly the heart was severed from its name,
each small chamber swept clean of memory.

Only pity laces my own heart like a boot
oddly bound and skips as if it was aged four.

Portrait of Valentine
After Roland Penrose

She has a mouth full of moths,
which take her breath under their wings.

Her words strive for the light's soul
but they must burn to in her skull.

Solitude has confused her lust
and dyed her face a drowned hue.

It is a navy-blue of separation
like a wild ocean, always bruised.

Her necklace is a wilted rosebush
crammed with clawing beads.

Her eyes, once almond shape
are hidden by gaudy butterflies

pinned to the head by the pupils.
The giddy colours are love's trophies.

But the creatures still flap their wings
and make her blind for real beauty.

The fancy parrots in her hair shriek
until she gives herself to the wind.

Geese

seem to have an endless lust for life

the snow goose in particular
sets the tone for winter
not without its limitations

flying high on goose liver

also caught on the breeze
of this life
Syringas from Persia

Nur Luft (just air)

* * *

the birds, distant blurs, crows or jackdaws
screaming in the wind
laments

Tempesta's lion growls at the nymph Cyane
witnessing abduction

contrast the colours of spring
a lake sheltered by verdant growth

two bushies in the undergrowth
where Z the Zephyr hides

the red red roses
the dark dark hyacinths
and the purple violets sweet

the landscape woodsy

De Raptu Proserpinae

my method is an example of *translatio*

the simple appropriation of a source

sweet sweet Sicily

★ ★ ★

Andromeda

Who would be a fly over Ethiopia
is menaced by sea-monsters
pirates play snap with her fingers
life is a noisy hungry struggle

———————————

When she saw him
she threw glances at his mouth
his eyes lucky charms
he kissed her wishing for much more

to delight her
to fulfil his desire

she clawed his flesh
sat upon his cock

she was carried away
(by two bushies?)
with her clothes left in the wind

his forehead wrinkled

she should have not gone so far
now in hot water

calling out for her friends
with dismay and growing alarm

* * *

Shadows

Shadows are omitted by Brueghel
but they are everywhere in Apollinaire's Calligrams
but paintings are not words
and words are not pictures
but what is *technopaignia* related to

to the smoke
to the smoking flames of war

the sound of snow in the nostrils
the rattle of trains across Europe, off to work

how can we make sense of the couples behaviour

the poem signals spatial and narrative discontinuities

but it contains a unification wherein poetical coherence lies
randomly distributed across the written surface

one is taken out of one's self
one feels estranged, unsettled
one no longer knows where one is

if you ask me they're having oral sex

there are no more familiar landmarks and
no more familiar custom posts

a passing herd, a cattle grid

letters (words) are paired and rhyming vignettes
are clustered and distributed
on such themes as
self-survival and conformity

it'   s
now
                        s

a train rattles through it
a town on the right
the country on the left
the picture divides into zones

a view of social cohesion and communal accord and
not a panorama of fracture and antagonism

or is it both
or vice versa

* * *

Borderland

We move on into a Mexican border of poetry
the desert is painted a sandy ochre and a burro plods its dry waste
the news forecasts storm

what is a good life (too late to now live one)
Mr Peck has made an existentialist error
killing is an engrained function of revenge
poverty seems natural

what is a border and whose is it
there is no war without warlords

the sovereign divides the plunder
dishes out the snake
rewards his acolytes
lavishes his greed and
commits no wrong

––––––––––––––––––––––––––––––––

They lived at Gander
where the Bishop had a hat
he had a knob on his castle and a cane

the first ones put out to sea in piss poor boats
waves of sea sprouts and water nymphs

and when they saw the sun they put up sail
and wore their boots
settled and called the place attractive

quite comfortable
having enough but longing the Mennonite
took a lover
and his wife took ill and died

October
what shall you wear my little one
grown old they landed
the boat up on to the shore

there they settled
and carried on farming after
their father's death

* * *

How is a fish shaped?
The petals blown off by the wind

Moose looting provides
rack of antlers for paddles
white pantaloon trousers

in all that snow
social services will provide a plough

to help maize grow they planted herring

they evolved that way
their scales an irruption of iridescence

mopped or rolled in oats (mouse?)
they make a tasty morsel

I couldn't live off moose or seal or whale

and Leif the Lucky called it
the land of grapes

Rachel McCarthy

Cd / Two followers of Cadmus devoured by a dragon

Stand far enough away
the bite could be a kiss,
the hand on the neck
an embrace.
In either case this moment
is about relenting.

I let you teach me about red;
cochineal, crimson, carmine lake;
how to crush bodies into pigment
the colour and texture of flesh;
how to blush;

that the perfect viewing distance
is a matter of mathematics
and perspective and the vanishing
point where I should start.
The tip of the spear
aimed at the heart.

Hg / Conjunctions

Cross my palm, I'll tell you about your past.
A handful of silver will buy you a flash
of a future.
Pull over.
Let me in.

I'm bringer of dreams, thief at the gates,
can you taste sulphur on my breasts, my face,

or the sour strip of gold on my lips
from clamping your hand—your five-fingered kiss—
to stifle guilt?

The ecstasy
of grief.

In less than nine weeks I've lost half my weight.
I've aged, my years are shorter than my days,
aphelion does not exist, the sun
is a plane mirror
between dawn and dusk,
cockerel, tortoise.
Shock waves are hollow mountains, shape calcified.
Traveller, leave your stone at the roadside.

Fe / Gauss's law for magnetism

The doctor holds out a model heart
half red, half blue,
a magnet drawing small arrows
of blood across its surface.

He twists the halves apart, like an avocado
from its stone, points to the tendon torn
from the ventricle wall, mimes the valve
opening, closing, closed.

Questions now are only academic,
of risk factors and genetics, matters
of replication; why one half pulls
and the other pulls away.

Pd / Lessons in stargazing: an epilogue

The night is cool and sharp with ozone,
like after a storm as the lodestones sink
and your compass trembles a new direction,
like that second before birds recall how they sing.

Now, like then, I pitch the telescope
screw the camera into place
adjust the focal length, open the shutter
wait.

Tell me about Newton, you said,
Galileo, about false halos, angles
of declination, how light weakens
passing through a lens. The failing
of our camera obscura.

I pointed out constellations;
Serpens Cauda, Pictor, Virgo.
The almost Earths that make us all so fierce.
Their signs of shift, the increasing distance
between one body and the next.

W / Little Red Riding Hood at dinner, age 55
(with sincerest apologies to Brandi Homan)

My lipstick is 'little red riding hood'
red, to distract from my last flush
of womanhood, the bluff
of my little red dress.

My grandmother was an expert
in the etiquette of loneliness,
still eating at her end of the table,
still sleeping on her side of the bed.

Stop me, if you're feeling uncomfortable,
we can talk about religion or war,
argue over the wine list, our set course
debate whether your knife could cut
me
open.

Honey, I'm your wolf in sheep's clothing,
so slip the loop of string from around
your finger when we leave.
Silver and stones will kill me.

City Winter

after Joan Mitchell

There's nothing more beautiful:
a smudge of taxis and buses
crawls across the empty grey; a muddle
of faces—lovers, long-lost friends—
rise to greet you. The mercury drops,
darkness yields to streetlights, headlights.
The edge of your known world.

What you've missed—
hidden behind the bright dome
of a church, the slashed glass
of an office block, massed clouds.
Last greens of summer
still in your head, a sudden recollection
of heat—*nothing more beautiful*

than knowing something is going
to be over. You walk the streets, the map
ingrained in your feet, stare
into uncurtained rooms
lit and ready for intimacies—
you've been outside yourself
too long. What you want

you won't find here. A train
leaves the city, its complicated tracks
weave past buildings still to be built,
girders lifting beyond the horizon,
its passengers bound for those lit rooms
flickering like grubby stars
on the outskirts.

Reading *Ulysses* in the Teri Aki Sushi Bar

He would have liked the concentric circles
of the California roll, whorls of salmon and avocado,
brightwhite rice, the ginger fanned
across the plate—like Molly Bloom,
her legs apart—the sake hot
in his throat, a trill of syllables.

He would have admired my discipline,
my quiet journey with Leopold
and tuna maki—squintyeyed
over the page, the words
running away from sense.

The Dublin streets are swollen with rain,
the delicate perfume of dung, and
there's a man hurrying home,
brown eyes saltblue, with no umbrella.
　　　　I will know him, oh yes, by the shrug
of his shoulders, hunch of his coat,
the way he looks up, suddenly,
comprehends

　　　　　　　that somewhere a girl, pretty,
captures a tiny creature in her chopsticks,
raises it to her lips, that first bite releasing
brine, bladderwrack, the green rot
of the ocean floor.
　　　　　　If only he
could sit across from her, worship
her perfect little teeth.

He will pass me on the street
one evening when the rain
smells like the ocean,

flame memory for an instant
before we turn our separate corners,
pull our collars to our throats.

The Russian Ending

We have no face
in the mirror, reader, we have no life
apart from the one you granted us
when you opened the book.

Turn the page. In the dead of winter, dead
of night, after a long illness, the last confession,
we release ourselves
to grief, a hard spring, a lost lover.

We ask you: what is wrong with our world,
with our hearts? Will we learn
to love again? Will we ever believe
in God, in redemption, in the parched earth?

Will our pain ever match
what happens in your world, where words
break on air like the rubble
of our homes? There is no end to it.

Castrati

All afternoon we argued this—
whether the voice became sweeter than roses,
a peasant transfixed by a hayrick,
hedges, hamlets, cathedral spires bathed in gilt
as the sound rotates,
ghostly at the lip of hills.
                                All afternoon
a cantata of finches in the veiled light,
fledgling, green, gold-tailed,
the honeyed flutter of their wings
in and out of our vision
as we talked of all those masterpieces;
the things we leave behind.

Because the Land is Barren

As though the rababa's pulse
comes from his aorta,

a nomad plucking out a muse
from the lute on his thigh;

melody that won't need
more than the lone string

to accompany his desert.

51

Foxes

The bass vocalist's genderless voice
merged us together.
Blue suit.
Blue sari.
Maybe it will always remain,
the crook of your elbow cupping mine.

The chandeliers lit up the room
as if it were still the Raj,
mellow on white upholstered chairs,
sparkling off glasses.
The floor was polished to shellac,
preserving every flex of dress-trousered leg
and whirling ankle.

When I think of you now
you seem constantly young,
your restless limbs embarrassed,
jerking and pulling to music. I don't want anymore
to press your lithe, fox-form
in my fern-embroidered sari,

but to release your odour
to the ululating cries in the scrub,
each voice taking the next one's pitch.

movements

six months later you visit the boats
seen daily from a distance and find nothing changed
only the height of grass and weed upon
the old slipway beside a crumbling boathouse

you find each vessel has not moved—
a little rustier they still sit out their days
tied to the bank—part overgrown quayside

here at low-tide you suspect they have not edged
an inch on their moorings

some fern grows between an anchor
and the hole it hangs from—only

this has happened—and some more rubbish
has been tipped between the boats and shore

the swans in the distance, the sand searching curlew
and black-headed gull further in are unconcerned—
move or remain still—its all the same to you and the birds

like Beatrice and Dante

everything is just peachy
to begin with around puberty
she knows nothing about him
or what his intentions might be
while he has only noticed the swells
of chest and butt that mark
her firmly as a woman
along the lines that nature intended
unless it changes its mind

as it does and she dies of some
disease that could now be treated
with little more than prescription
drugs to make the difference
between life and death and the
comedy being written—but such
is the comedy for there is no
tragedy as no deal is ever struck
that says you will get what
you want—that is the laugh of it
there is a divinity in life
walks off the page at you
has a beginning middle and end
but no plot

the kind of knowing

knowing like and unlike
samples of vignettes
begin with the assumption
practitioners know more than they say
most of which is tacit
a capacity for reflection
in the midst of action
to cope with the unique / uncertain
a kind of rigor
like and unlike
derived from myths about the relations
we create for ourselves
for future interaction
touch on very lightly

Hallucinating like Circe

This is true night.

After the moon slinks behind a cloud
the walls move closer

to hear me breathe.

The ground trembles,
the trees in the garden turn white

their roots dig up bones
for rats to gnaw.

And rising from the slime,
creatures,

fangs, fur, prowling.

The night menaces
in and out of my dreams

on soft pads.

My lips melt.
I am silent as light.

Bright blue flames spark
from the pillow

to the tinder of my hair.

In the kitchen, pots of herbs
are awash with my blood.

At Callanish Standing Stones

I slip through an unseen doorway
between ransacked grave

and solid rock. Up. I am wisp of cirrus
in this golden eagle land

where a woman, carrying the weight
of camera, tripod and who she once was,

takes a photo in black and white
keeping still for the long exposure

as if light holds the key to existence.
A drunk waits for a boat by the loch.

Stones refuse to bow down
but lean towards the harvest moon.

This tip was broken off,
shoved into a wall. Cuckoo rock.

I am coming back to myself.
Away from silvery myths,

back to the wandering of strangers,
the air layered with others' lives—

we breathe them in, never knowing.
It's noon. If I stare hard enough into the sky

I can see the stars.

propeller/Le Corbusier

as the propeller
slices the thigh
of his swimming form/

Le Corbusier is reminded
that machines are not just
for living in
but for dying
under as well

he might surface
in the wash
of a boat's violent remark

holding together
with blood irony
how his leg can be
undesigned

he realises buildings
should not be
photographed
until flesh
has fallen
off their bones

when we realise

we walk to the back of a mind
and sit down
to face each other

when we realise

we walk to the back of a mind
and sit down
to face each other

when we realise

we walk to the back of a mind
and sit down
to face each other

when we realise

we walk to the back of a mind
and sit down
to face each other

only before

this fly was on my hand
not yours

Three Songs of the Inarticulate

Song of the Dodo
(Mare aux Songes)

doo-doo doo-doo
doo-doo doo-doo

fish fruit stone
fruit fish stone
stone fruit fish
fish stone fruit
fruit stone fish
stone fish fruit

fruit fruit fruit

doo-doo doo-doo
doo-doo
doo
doo

Song of the William Morris Wallpaper

black bird black bird black bird
drib kcalb drib kcalb drib kcalb

open beak   closed beak
closed beak   open beak

f o l
i
a g e

bird   berry   straw   berry   bird

black bird black bird black bird

Song for Peter who has no speech (or movement)

Mmm
Mmm
Mmm *(hungry)*
Mmm *(angry)*
Mmm *(crying)*
Mmm *(because you are in bed and the
curtain hanging in the bar of light from
the landing resembles a man in a rain
coat with a fedora pulled over his eyes
and moves—hardly perceptibly—every
few minutes).*

dragonfly

the smallest sounds:

> a snail rasping cells
> from an ivy leaf,
> sparrow's claws
> in a broken wall;

> the dragonfly's clasp
> as it swings
> over the lawn,
> clicking like a trap:

> *look at me who
> threw nothing away.
> If your song survives
> a fraction of my time,
> if your species lives as long,*

> *then*

from Claim (a map, a catalogue, a questioning)

In the dream there are boxes of cardboard and wood, suitcases made of leather and canvas, bags of woven plastic. There are objects strewn everywhere: patterned scarves, balls of yarn, stacks of index cards and blankets, mismatched pairs of shoes. She does not know where time is coming from or where it is fast escaping, but she feels it beating wings against her, flickering all around. Her hands are only two, scrambling to tuck objects into boxes, into bags. First the yarn and then a shoe, then a bottle and removing the yarn, a sweater and two books, she rearranges the shoes, realizing there are three, begins sifting her hands through the mess in search of another pair. Time jeering silent insistence, she folds objects away. Positioning, stacking, arrange again. She closes containers one by one, sealing flaps of boxes, pulling zippers of suitcases, clipping shut the buttons of bags.

★

Dear Nation,
What anchors, what milk, what murmur of mine?

Dear Immigrant,
Shouldered loyalties, what offered up for entry. Shout
softly from safe rooftops.
Claim skin, claim map, claim mobile.

★

Cream-colored portrait, {Jerusalem}1955: she stands beside her sister.
A doll lies face down on her sister's lap. Her hands poise over the body,
talons curl the torso, invent a spine.

She picks. Perforates. Fingers pull skin from nail.
My mother's hands move incessantly; their resting mode a clickety fidget.
Conversation drilled in snaps, split tick, insistent metronome.

Twenty years later, she is graduating from architecture school {Montreal}:
clutching her diploma, rolled and ribbon-sealed. Fingers coil like un-
bloomed ferns, tendons tense, exposed.

Fleck memory, name distant sound, what carpus, nails, reveal.
Terse the knuckle. Split edges, ringlet, ridge

*I dream about the toys I left behind in Romania, Stuffed bears, lions, cotton
dresses.*

At the table, her fingers flutter over, graze silverware, slide long mouth of
the wine glass.

*

Where is the road?
parrot voice, 1950, inflections lip Italian, sea sounds from Genoa to
Venezuela

born into the ear-curl, easternmost
Košice, Slovakia, province of Gemer

Dear Immigrant:
You'll find no war here.

Grossman to Gömöri, passport changed (false) to Gemersky,

a name with no record

first thing he did was wire the 300 back

railroad division, where you had to become a card-carrying member

escapee's roulette table: Australia, New Zealand, United States,
Venezuela, Canada

The year he sold ties on Vienna streets, fading credentials

Wait for boat. Dock family, son

"He would be very proud, he'd sell ties for a day, then buy me a banana.
That was a big thing."

water flowed in when it rained

the three wives (also) worked full time

The custom of sending college-age children abroad

Playing tennis with the listening. Rich kids "down so pat." Picked it up.

dust swills up on the landing dock, hot dust, touch foot to anchored
ground

What carried between continents?

Dear Immigrant:
Complexion marks a perfect score. Lighter is righter.
Welcome from, raise stakes, take home, fair game.

inscribed, an eyelash curled into the pelvic bulge, a ghost-child
suckling marrow

1946, Košice— A woman arrives at Ila Mitros's house for a gathering.
Hair Slovak-wet, jaw-line a knifing slick. Their glance across the room
at one another.

"After the war, a fever to meet and marry"

"Didn't want to go to Israel, didn't want to be those Jews"

Moved to Bella Monte 1951
Moved to San Bernardino 1953 opened manufacturing company

a country good to them

for textiles (shmates), interior traveled in tricycle plane

Dear Immigrant:
Try on the tongues. Shout softly from safe rooftops.
Good neighborhood, good neighbor.

in the bedroom they all shared, his skin dense now with tropic smog

a name with no record

1958 "we really had made it." Castro on the new television. He thinks
"I'll send my son to school"

Dear Immigrant,
Put up for rent. Claim noun. Claim number.

                                          "I liked the meritocracy"

befriended soldiers, loved potatoes   "saved his life"

Diffused mines   "You could always spare a Jew"

Rimavská Sobota— E Slovakia. He is born.

for the little knobby legs

To tell her that he loved her

1945—labor camp liberated. Return.

Who are the communists.   "didn't want to be *those Jews*"

asthmatic bronchitis   Familia Stark   arrhythmia   shtetl Perbenyc

aspirated in Auschwitz munitions   return to Košice

a name with no record

1951 Slánský Trials — all government Jews sentenced to jail

"They never wanted to be part of the Caracas community. *Those Jews.*"

To tell her that he loved her

                                   Dear Immigrant,
                    Your place in the man, woman of things.

A Starkness in the Late Afternoon

afternoon light   on stone   is immediacy
thought or   in itself
immaculate unsundering

the geese's flight   their warm
indivisible bodies   as much as   on the path
coarse stone   a single feather

and here I go   tearing the quilt
apart   patch by patch   all parts
no one   no one will love

on the storm-   fed sea   the wrath
the men and I   all prey to
praying to   the sea god

the high waves could be   suppose it
myrmidons   unnamed abettors
our fear   unchanged unchanneled

our prayers   scattered invisible

Prairie

sprawling through night   a train's low horn
the crossings   empty   the ritual
maintained   reflex or   especial precaution

do the sleepers hear it   do their ears
make unconscious record   to litanize

prescience loses particularity   unbound
on prairie   to vague expectation
with or without   hope

with or without   the train whistle's
thread   reminder redeemer

of silence   each isolate mind
banked in prescience   if it's not nostalgia
impalpable   in small hours   impalpable

in the drift   as names ease from objects
unmannered ritual   especial   withoutness

(T)here

there I sang   always the equation   plenitude and
absence   daffodils a whole bobbing field
learning to disjoin   thoughtless   careless

count and catalogue   your prosthetic limbs
lightning as the   ever-lagging illumination
of sound   down in the syllable   grunt and sway

a Saturday night   a beckoning thunder
there I had   without complacency   pleasure
a song a hymn   one man's chant

Saturday the pubs the   revving motorcycles
loudness   acceptably enjoyed   plenitude always
thoughtless   another attention   an ever sway

Midnight

the fierce clasp   in the arc
with its own memory   can't simulate
flame   can't simul   deliquesce

would that I   is purity separable
from virtue   is the clasp
                              virtuous

tissue and skin and bone   loved
my only   not flame   not only
surfeit   comes down to infrastructure

come down   one drop one
fierce   with its own memory
a spell   and its yield

adept adrift   deliquesce
my surfeit of virtue   flame
the arc the drop   can't   can't own

Richard Berengarten

Selections from 2^6 — Two to the Power of Six
a work-in-progress based on Yi Jing

After the massacre

Mouth of a dead shoe
squeaks toothless out of clay.
No those aren't vultures

they're jays, said
the Chairman. Be
careful with that spade.

Both local magnolias
and jacarandas have
been burned here.

Permaplastoid froth
covers and seals the pools.
A silver chain was

surrounded by several
connected vertebrae, reported
the bespectacled young forensic

archaeologist, wearing
a blue hamsah medallion
around her slender throat.

She sweeps shadows

She sweeps shadow
from oblong flagstones,
square tiled walls

and straight-planked
floors. Careful
to spill no single

speck, she collects
shadow-dusts
in an angled pan

whose contents
she tips in
a black silk bag

tied with plaited
flame-coloured
strings. Each

evening she does this
and spills the bag
across night.

Inflate nothing

Everything you've ever
thought, been and done
will fit on a small shelf,

nay button, pray-you,
to be undone, pinhead,
microchip. So, Caesar,

inflate nothing. However
many millions of foes
imagined or real, you

exterminated, however
deep and long the ranks
of warriors and horses,

boned or stoned,
you busied and buried
with you, emperors

perish like
any man, like
Everyman.

At least one of the liars

At least one
of the liars has
gone back to her

own homestead
on the other
side of Paradise

Island. For the time
being at least
we are free

from her malice
rippling and rocking
foundations of

our trust, but
not for long. Be
aware she'll return

in guise of
a cute sincere
spontaneous friend.

Consultation of the diagrams

Consultation
of the diagrams
is helpful

in the construction
of hypotheses, buildings
and voyages,

in the precise
locating of wells, mines,
mirrors, towers,

in alleviating
insomnia and fears
of death,

in the correct
turning of antennae
towards origins

and in all forms of
measurement and modes
of harmonising.

A student

So lacking in confidence
she has no idea how
bright and clever she

really is. And all this
fineness has appeared
as if from nowhere. Other

members of her
family had excelled at
nothing spectacular or

even special before they
were wiped out—mother by
disease, father in a car crash,

both brothers in a
seawreck. In her wide
pupils this history

is pooled. Otherwise she
appears all future, scant
presence, no past.

Poem for Gully

Your path, you choose,
that chooses you, is
good, honourable, true,

for yourself you test
and probe at every
step. Commending that,

what least I ask myself
is mediation of
perfectionist desire with

attentiveness to undercurrents
and shadows. In their wellings
and among their interstices

so long as we keep questioning
each other and ourselves
we might get through and

under clichés that waylay
and even blind us among
blander lightfilled spaces.

Concerning archaeology

A cat's jaw poked
up from the reed bed, slimed
with mildew and moss.

On the old battlefield
I found half a button, and
she, a pottery fragment.

Josh's fossil turned out
a nautiloid, black limestone,
400 million years old.

Air in these lungs
is thick with crumbled
shit dust. Meanings

that moan in dross
and memorabilia demand
magnified attention. We

traverse the field in
more and slower detail
to get anywhere at all.

A good general 1

A strong swimmer in
swirling currents, he
saved eight others from

drowning as they crossed
two rivers, fleeing their
bombed village. Three more

perished, shot crossing
scrubland, including his
youngest brother. The six

who came through lay down
and wept beneath bushes
and in crevasses. That night

he sat apart, his back against
a cliff-face, saying nothing and
watching stars. Once over

the border he drilled and
disciplined his men and taught
them skills of killing.

A good general 2

No charismatic
demagogue, he made
sure first to look after

his own and hone
their judgements and
speeds in strategy. He

deepened their
trusts and loyalties.
not only to himself but

one another. They repaid
him by following and
honouring him all his

life long. Strangers said it
was they who made him
a good general. To his

end he remained
modest, with a dry
understated humour.

Worship Tendency

my hands, white from the chill
turn black against the rising sun
heavy with nothingness
the way a tower bears the weight of its bricks

this is not time
but the end of time   falling into
the small of your hand—
curved   shadow on the half moon

as day bleeds into night and night into day
my consciousness is not broken from yours

in this union— temperance, forbearance
two days of chanting
the sound becomes a bridge
made richer by the chasm beneath

this rhythm I thought our own—
counterpoint to a prayer sung
6000 years ago
or before
a moon,   cyclic
the edge of a disease

in this weight, the weightlessness
of the stone that brings down the mountain
gathering speed
molten lava and the wet earth
we will not inherit

I ask for strength
something you say
cannot be given
but must be found

the first birdcall of the night is the last—
an altar for the city

the god of this woods
carved into stone,
artefact of holy light
I wake to at moments
like water returned to the sea

it is always the same side of the moon that we witness

the desire to worship
a prerequisite of our faith

this time of inbetween passes
like the shadow of a cloud
and it is my own voice that rings out
into the hollow
a reverberation like breath
in the walls of the lungs,
but larger—
          a stratosphere

truth is found again in detail
the difference between worship and prayer

for example, there is ice only in the deepest craters of the moon
and only in crevices untouched by light
and even this is uncertain

moonshine, you say, is more than just reflection

my fast— a hallucinogen
that empties me of repetition
so that now is only the now
undecided

I hold it   weeping

star-struck,
lunatic
beautiful new every
from the time I still loved
born again
in these hands

Second Waking (from part II)

in a moment of fatigue, a single inhalation
catching a germ on a breeze

can spark an epidemic
the moment air becomes breath becomes air again

sometimes the only way out
is back from where we came

                  ~

I wake to cold coffee, a muffin wrapper
yesterday's stale croissant
your mug, still dry on the table
this air that was already breathed—musty
after a night's sleep with the window closed

                  ~

dear lover,
I want to meet you

in a city where the sun
shines through the haze
and people are walking with nowhere to go
and there is nothing I feel that can't be said
and nothing that has to be done

I tell you, you are too beautiful for this world
but you are hanging the laundry, running downstairs,
you are laughing, opening the door
you are in it, and from where I'm standing
I don't understand the difference

~

there is something in my blood,
spinning, pining, pulling me to you

the hunger for food and a hunger
remembered outside of walls

I stand too quickly and it all
rushes from my head—

sudden asphyxiation, as if breath
was something that happened, an occasion
like toast in morning or sunset

there is something in my blood—a ghost, a chime
an echo of what might have been

had I really met you

~

all of 'you'

~

this time   at sea
waves cling to the side of the boat
somewhere on the ocean floor   a life
we are not even aware of
mist rises from the caldera
the smell of sulphur, and cliff-top—
fragments of a lost civilisation

~

the other side of the world turns to smoke
this night is only inside our brain
desired shift in consciousness
a sudden
                    attack of the heart
cicadas shriek in the neon lights and we
hand in hand, intoxicated, believe this is morning

~

everyday the world grows larger
I can no longer find you
your god is dead, and mine—
this false prophecy
belonging to no one   and everyone
is proof of our weakness

~

when we meet again it's autumn, a concert in a park,
a 10-foot screen   song   and you—
            the stillness beneath it
piano   a kalimba   a voice   merlot disguised in a bag
arpeggios cascade the treble
    and the bass   its own rhythm
    rides the avalanche,   in an instant
overtakes it—   rush of feather and stone
—syncopation—
now:
            a mill   a pasture   fields of rice and tea
a woman driving a cart,   her husband behind her and a lame mule
that won't run fast enough to save him
just one moment   or another   lived-out
  non-consecutively
  beneath the same sky
this ground we sit on
still wet with yesterday's rain

Craig Watson

Wake Up, Dead Man

A man who was in love climbs into the canopy hoping his bones become branches and his skin turn to leaves. What if we never die, he thinks, because we are never fully living.

In reality, the forest is a murderous tangle of ridges and deep crevasses, deceitfully covered by the sun. Ghosts roll up from someone else's sleep, their hunger forms your life. Fascists advance from one small insurrection to another.

Even the conscious could wait here, scratching the surface of time, producing more calendars.

Waves recoil from citation, each believing that it is the last swell ever born.

Hurdy Gurdy Porn Sonnet

I can't stop grinding
Old milk lures the dead
Now stop seducing
Conjunctions on a frontier
Keys come and go
The peasant works transparent
Hard-wired inadequacies
Singing "sex, money and
Left for Siberia"
How long will you wait
Even the worst person in the world
Metastasized to orgasm
Words surpass words
Or so said the words

St. James Infirmary

Well Otis Redding told my mother
Don't even think of breeding here
Beauty only drinks the dirt
To which sacrifice adheres

I saw my lost love Crow Jane
Dancing down Fannin Street
I had sworn to bless and worship her
Then put a bullet in her meat

Minutes track like hours
Hours fail the days
Every night my soul escapes
From a body that won't decay

I rode that train to hell
Further than anyone had been before
But the gods sent me back with a mirror
And a list of everything to ignore

Radio Faucet

it's so beautiful here I don't know who to punish which is funny because
we're not allowed to touch so there's no way to tell a good act from a
bad don't even try to tell me the names of your destitute there are no
spectators here and every tombstone diminishes its reference in receding
halves that snake like roots to crag the walls and knot in crotches so it's
impossible to climb the ladder that delivered us even with strangled
hands which turn to flowers as we all huddle in a chicken-bone house
and wait for news of that we have been forgotten and are free

Douglas Messerli

changing hands

David Bromige *Threads* (Los Angeles: Black Sparrow Press, 1971)
David Bromige *My Poetry* (Berkeley: The Figures, 1980)
David Bromige *Desire: Selected Poems 1963–1987* (Santa Barbara: Black Sparrow Press, 1988)
David Bromige *The Harbormaster of Hong Kong* (Los Angeles: Sun & Moon Press, 1993)

On June 3 of this year, poet David Bromige died at his home in Sebastopol, California, of complications from diabetes, a stroke and heart attack. During his last years, according to friends such as D. A. Powell, Bromige suffered from "dementia."

How different the David Bromige I knew in the 1990s, the time when I first met him—if I remember correctly, at a reading of his in New York City—publishing his book, *The Harbormaster of Hong Kong* (the title poem is still one of my favorite of his works) in 1993. The following year, David appeared at a literary salon in the Sun & Moon offices on September 22, and read, I believe, that same weekend at Beyond Baroque in Venice. In those days he was the very image of a clever, stunningly quick-witted punster, creating his famed maxims and dicta, many of which dotted his poems, seemingly out of clear air: "There is no revision in the grave," "Lambs live a long time in our recipes," "Every endless summer hurries in a fall." Many of these were presented in the form of "pairings" of lines which in their oppositional syntax nonetheless paralleled and defined the other:

infatuation

_____
break break break
on thy cold gray stones o shore

kiss me quick

_____
too late

Bromige was what at one time would be described as a wit, and his poetry literally shimmered with his quick connections, or, at the other extreme (as in "You") revealing a slow, "deliberate" process, where the reader, working with the author, moved through the matter of the poem, "changing hands," so to speak, with the author as together they made their way through the work. But these are only two aspects of a body of writing that was constantly in shift, moving between narrative and lyricism, rhyme and radical disassociation at the drop of a hat, sometimes, as in 'In an Orchard, in America, in August,' focusing on the lush surfaces of things in order to reveal their inner core:

> Let this be
> the story of the core.
> The part that's thrown away,
> that can't be used.
> That can't speak for itself,

Bromige's quick shifts in syntax and genre clearly irritated some, particularly poets and readers who demanded a signature style from a writer. I remember attending Bromige's reading at Beyond Baroque where I sat next the usually fair-minded poet-editor Lee Hickman, with Hickman hissing into my ear, "I just can't stand this kind of writing." Hickman was an often obstinate critic, but here I suspect it was just Bromige's wide poetic range and abilities that irritated him—and so delighted me.

Born in London in 1933, Bromige grew up with signs of becoming tubercular, and was sent to an isolation hospital for four months as a child. His second childhood "trauma" was his existence in London during the Blitz, during which, on one particular night, a series of neighborhood bombs seemed likely to destroy their family home. After the war Bromige won a scholarship to Haberdashers' Aske's Hampstead School, but after completing his certificate he took a job on a dairy farm in southern Sweden. Soon after, he emigrated to Canada, living for a while in Saskatchewan, Ontario, and Alberta, before moving to Vancouver to be near to his sister, and where he attended the University of British Columbia, meeting poets such as George Bowering, Frank Davey, Robert Creeley, Charles Olson, Denise Levertov, and Robert Duncan, who might be described as Bromige's mentor.

In 1962 Bromige won a Woodrow Wilson Scholarship, which required he do his graduate work in a different university. Accordingly, Bromige chose the University of California at Berkeley, moving to the Bay area. From 1970 on he became a Professor of Literature at Sonoma State University. His poetry collection of 1988, *Desire: Selected Poems, 1963–1987*, won the Western States Book Award.

Many of his students have described David as a caring and giving teacher. As D. A. Powell wrote soon after his death:

> Our classroom was in the theatre department, and it was furnished with ungodly dilapidated sofas . . . So each week we'd sprawl on the sagging couches, reading poems reproduced in purple ink on a ditto machine, and David would sit cross-legged in the center of the room, sigh deeply, smile, and praise even the most sickly poems, though he often seemed to pass first through a period of deep physical pain before he'd bless us with that smile and praise.

I did not know David Bromige well; apart from working with him on the one book we published, attending three readings, and working with him on his selection of poems from *From the Other Side of the Century: A New American Poetry 1960–1990* we seldom communicated over the years. Yet I sensed in David a similar openness and a complete commitment to living.

As we left my offices to take him to the airport, David called out to my companion Howard, "Please, you have to get a photograph of the two of us in front of Sun & Moon. Here, Douglas, let us hold hands." We did, the camera catching us in the act of "changing hands."

Los Angeles
November 20, 2009

Swantje Lichtenstein   *translated by Kevin Perryman*

THE PRISMATIC cloudlet
gaia or I reveal you
want to pull the blanket over it

the private parts best
held back cowardly they pull off
the fig-leaf, these smuggled words

changing questions of genre
shoot through the extremities
of the body believed dead

in the tonic waterfall
from the source of the spring
taut up-river

to be jumped over on
the increase and stepped across:
out of tune in no key

from leg right up to head
a rustling and dreaming

is close and hold vigil, too
hold vigil all night.

from the cycle **Along the Living Line**

Someone from Säckingen, a liar,
since he has no horns,
as a diabolical horse-force-feeder and hot-chocolate-drinker says,
dies of putrescence of the body,
puts blond curls in little boxes,
sniffs at medicinal substances,
slays the know-it-alls with his sword
and then knocks at their doors

betraying for want of mimicry in front
or a sting behind,
relies on letters and sounds,
recognizes the Dionysian side of this art
and at the way out puts up no resistance
to the way.

Dialogue Between a Door and the Room,
the surrounding walls they tile the clay white
under the wind-glad set-squares awaiting their alternate turn,
crept along the draught on the floorboard
footlike they claw into the floor,
corresponding with the wallpaper under the lamp
in the room about the track, about the windows.
At the mooring the indifferent consonants sit,
with the cipher-sound under lock and key, they pinch the voice,
undrawn, they outlast the silence, the guttural.

The book is right,
in German vineyards there were ladders
hanging on the hilltop on the rock face
green sprouting under the ground
life writhes round the angular
My face fights its steep
way up to the ruins,
collecting points and welts,
lustre and radiance choose where
they want to be themselves
and more and more houses
grow along the rivers.

From the cycle At the Hour of Horae

Full-moon-coloured land, raspberry house with a silver roof
in the end an obstacle can always be found, as long as day,
as long as day grabs at the ends of this earth, we reach
each field's four corners, radiant grey and lovingly yellow.

In among the brambles there are urns and stones
towering up into new complexes next to the wooden
shack that received us with dancing and in the fairy-tale forest
I kneel down and pick a piece of futility.

Dependent, we spin into night, holding onto the children's hands,
the earth withdraws into hollows, our legs are stuck
on the fire the rice pudding bubbles, the insects crack,
into the landscape power and clemency launch themselves jointly.

he holds his hand over it, shovels light into the shade.
Leasehold land on the human hills
weeps and drips air from the pores of my skin,
softness reflects on the Transistrian flag.

The driver taking us to the graves,
with his hand he pushed his hair from his forehead,
and then shook his head, unsteady on his
high heels all the way down his smoothly ironed clothes.

The first hill full, —filled with graves, on the second floor
the stone is skew, grass growing over the books and hands,
I tread in deep cracks between them, hanging onto the bars,
swing myself onto the next one and thereunder am lost.

We stand facing each other and bridge that glance,
the sound melts and the points reach back,
touching sight in shaking gestures,
hang on skin's wickerwork, don't miss each other,

hoist the colours with the big mouths,
in the flames licking at the edge of the lake.
Sunflowers wreathed in black stones
soak the open ducts of the lower eyelid.

No one notices, everyone sees the dilution,
mumbling you bend down to the ear of the hearer,
mention the bleak borders of the note
as long, as long as you're in the encounter, go on.

fighting for darker eyes, a stab in this gentleness,
competitive bets beat the knee into bending,
teach the set-square cunning, the wall the inflexibility of sharp bends,
hemmed in, we dither, looking for a mouse-hole,

a magpie nest in the crowing poets' bird-house
mine, no, mine, no, I, I, I, the flapping roars.
Gentle glow of the hardness, through the face twice not an
arched beam the breadth heals over into nothing,

an elliptical encounter, circling scorn
wipes that smile off his face to the white noise
among the deaf the pensive hills are alive,
throw those hard berries to the blind.

Intervene and confuse, hold tight and make a din,
your plan doesn't surprise me, is most revealing
making me shout, scream, lisp, stutter, dribble, act,
under the turban I hide the desserts of

emigrés, in the layers alphabets, a pen in the knot
and draw a line on which the words then sit.
We swap them and smile at the end of the reef,
mistaking the net for the spider, weaving at the loom,

embroidering, the needle breaks in your foot, travelling inside you
in your nearest you wake up again and eavesdrop at
white walls, place the set-square in the corners
and search for the hinge that promises colours.

Gertrud Kolmar

translated by philip kuhn & ruth von zimmermann

Borzoi

Yours was the darkness, the cavern of the mother-body.
Yours was the ground, the earth that carries animals.
You crawled around blind, seeking and sucking
    under the teats of the bitch
And nourished yourself, grew and became seeing
And played between brothers and sisters . . .
Do you still remember?
No you don't remember anything anymore:
You hardly know this coat that flows upon you, white-fluffy
    foaming sea, around isabel-coloured islands.

Lovely One, graceful One, with the slender stretched head, the gentle,
    brown gleaming almond eyes,
You dream
Northern pale birches on the moor, from which the blackish burnt
    monster the shovel-horned elk, blazes forth.
Your blood
Still hounding the grey wolf through pine darkness of Russian forests,
Still tracking grazing reindeer-herds across moss and lichen
    of the tundra,
Still hearing the fearful wailing, the lamenting cry of the snow hare
Before the huntsman . . .

By day
You rest silently on the rug and with the gentleness of the hind,
    the unicorn, lift your woman's face towards me,
Or you run head down, like dogs do, sniffing and scratching
    at the compost mounds, bushes and borders.

In autumn nights,
When stronger, colder stars flicker,
Occasional drip resounds falling off the tree,
When yellowing grass breathes freshness and moistness,
I pull the coat around my shoulders, open the iron door
Of the garden;

You chase in colossal bounds.
You fly, you spatter
Like a snowstorm over the carpet of withered dripping leaves;
Silver fluttering flame, your mane-like tail flares after you.
And I go and call you with more muffled voice, and you alert, tall
    and light, ghost-pale, a silhouette by the turn of the road.
You stand and stare.
What do you descry?
Did yellow eyes glimmer by the alder-buckthorn, in the honeysuckle
    bushes, cats eyes, which you hate?
Is a ghost stepping towards you, fluttering hands full of bloody offal—
    and your long nose sniffs the prey?
Are you just home to a foreign, incomprehensible soul,
    which at times leaves the animal house as a beingless transparent
    shell?

She roams
Over the lawns, between the bronze chrysanthemums, and you wait
    for the return.
Is she approaching?
My fingers touch the coolness and smoothness of the lizard-forehead . . .
    a collar tinkles.
Obedient beside me, the pale and silent companion trots homeward.

The Angel in the Forest

Give me your hand, the dear hand, and come with me;
Because we want to walk away from the people.
They are small and wicked, and their small wickedness
    detests and torments us,
Their spiteful eyes creep around our face, and their greedy
    ear gropes the word of our mouth.
They gather henbane . . .
So let us flee
To the meditative fields, which congenially console
    our roaming feet with flowers and grass,

To the river, patiently bearing on its back heaving burdens, heavy
     freight-bursting ships,
To the animals of the forest who don't speak evil.

Come.
Autumn mist veils and dampens the moss with
     a dull emerald glow.
Beech leaves roll, an abundance of gold-brown coins.
In front of our steps leaps a red quivering flame,
     the squirrel.
By the mire black winding alder lick upwards
     into copper evening splendour.

Come.
Because the sun has crept down into its hollow, and
     its warm reddish breath has floated away.
Now a vault opens up.
Under its grey-blue arc, between crowned columns of trees,
     the angel will stand,
Tall and slender without wings.
His countenance is sorrow.
And his robe has the pallor of icy gleaming stars
     in winter nights.
The Being,
Who does not speak, no should, he just is,
Who knows no curse, brings no blessings and does not
     surge into cities, towards that which dies:
He does not behold us
In his silver silence.
But we behold him,
Because we are two and forsaken.

Perhaps
A brown faded leaf blows against his shoulder,
     slides down;
We want to pick this up and keep it, before we move on.

Come with me, my friend, come.
The stairs in my father's house are dark and crooked
      and narrow, and the steps are worn;
But now it is the house of the orphan, and strangers
      live in it.
Take me away.
The old rusty key in the gate hardly obeys my feeble hands.
Now it creaks shut.
Now look at me in the darkness, you, from today
      my home.
Because your arms shall build me sheltering walls,
And your heart will be my chamber and your eye my window
      through which the morning shines.
And the forehead towers up as you stride.
You are my house on all the streets of the world, in every
      valley, on every hill.
You roof, you will thirst wearily with me under sweltering midday,
      shiver with me when snow storm whips.
We will thirst and hunger, suffer together,
Together, one day, sink down by the dusty wayside verge
      and weep . . .

The Urals

When I seize darkness, jagged edges wound
My hand.
There are mountains which rise and buck with spikes
      and crevasses like the crest of a dragon.
There are the Urals.
Chain from North to South, division between West and East,
      wall between two worlds.
I must put out the lamp, so that it might become, so that it might
      crawl in front of me, immense lizard-being, in night.
For its rocks swell, and its forests grow
Out of my soul.

And the breath of my mouth weaves smokily over the snow
    of the Jaman-tau,[1] my eternal summit.

I muse.

Clumsy, shaggy bears lollop out of caves, growling,
Wolf-noses sniff in marsh-land,
Brown furry sable-martens slink.
Myself, I created the shocking feathery yellow-eyed
    owl face
And the great silver-grey fish for the leaping flowing source
And the heavy wing flapping woodland grouse
    for the black forests,
Which, again and again, the golden talons of my rock eagle
    smite and rip apart into air . . .
But the root of the great dusk-maned pine tree thrusts
    into the depths, penetrates eyeless blind towards inexhaustible
    chambers, towards stacked, heaped treasures,
Which are green: snake skinned serpentine, viper under
    the stones, and malachite like fossilised leaves
And brighter chrysoprase, which must not see the sun that
    avariciously sucks and fades its apple splendour.
Precious minerals shimmer; scattered ruby seeds lure the bills
    of underground hammer-headed birds.
Almond stones ripen, filled with colourful agate; chalcedony
    swells grape-like;
And brown marble, scattered with orange shells, dawns . . .

All of that is beautiful.

But I also have the other, unfavourable, lacklustre:
Shadow gullets, where the misshaped one squats, half creature,
    which escaped me before I gave it pulsating life.
Mute, suffocated, it screams for me, but I shudder;
    I do not look down.
It waits for redemption . . .
Once, maybe once
In cold starless gloominess,

When wind-night whistles softly like a monstrous grey rat,
When tree stumps, rotten stubs of teeth, chew in the mouth
  of the earth,
When flakes spread ghostly shrouds for the dead high moor—
Then I will go there,
My hands on trembling breast, and bend towards the abyss . . .

[1] The highest mountain in the Southern Urals is Jaman-Tau (1640 m).

Ziba Karbassi   *translated by Stephen Watts & Ziba Karbassi*

I Have Poured Myself To The Wind

A curl of the eyelash a furl of the lips and with two bitter almonds
            in your face   your face scarred to the bone by a brand
If you cut into my skin you will know what I'm saying There's a line
            through this writing looks like it's burnt

Truth or lies I don't know I only know you and this that whenever I'm
returning from you my hand becomes frozen and I walk exaggeratedly
exactly like now when the pen doesn't fit well in my hand and the word
like a thread winds about the feet of my lines and your eye's almond
flips over onto my skirt and stares out at me from there bitterly

There is no way back, I have decanted myself to the winds up to my waist
and nothing in anything of me can be put back for you again And the world
is a severed bridge that cannot carry anyone across to anyone any longer
and from all the corners of a few houses just a few pillars without cornice or
plinth remain swaying in mid-air I am the explorer of the breath that I have
plummeted down I have fallen in love with breathlessness and of a sudden
in this air-deprived atmosphere I have become the breather of all breath

And the sun and the snow mountains and the bullfinch that flies from that
branch of the tree where we once lay and everything moves from anywhere
and everything flies from any place and everyone from anywhere dead or alive,
all all all of them breathe from inside me even love when it becomes short of
breath takes its needy gasps from me

Where are you going from me   where am I gone   what does this mean?

And when you shackle my feet and . . .
With shackled feet I have been dancing all the way with those shackled feet
I have come dancing from the tops of unnamed graves and I know the names
of the dead ones one by one and by heart like my pearl drops of rain

Where, where can you wrap rope, chains, roads around my voice-breath?

'Say it' I said 'Say it' Say my name and put its end-stop End it Ok

Collage Poem: 10

Its only the spells on my lips that are witches these holy
waters they cannot rise my dear how you are that you are
such blue water and you are able to rise up from my fire
and you come to my embrace and you don't melt

How are you that you are so suddenly pulling my legs down
from dancing in the air close up my lips with your smile &
opening from my navel how you fly out & away my little dove
how you're tearing that eagle to pieces to again make a mirror
from my knee-shine without me & the water & the mirror what
are you doing if you come into the lip-laugh between my thighs
how are you going to cry out while we laugh-cry each other

How are you that you are not cheek-to-cheek with me yet you
are closer than my two cheeks and me not there at all how you
are that you are a fire that blossoms out of my hand from the
whole of me a fire that's trotted off that you've tethered your
horse to to a horse that is floating like a wave from burgundy
silk that's pulped to a pomegranate picking a garden of pome-
granates & pocketing them how naked you're leaving me now
without horse wave or red fruit without coming you've come
already walking into my valleys from far off

Turning my grandmother's wine back to grapes again you put
them on a silver salver on the table for me so that I'd never now
drink wine or sadness sadness that is greater even than all this
where shall I put you you putting me that's you putting me off
from yourself and where might that be

When you are coming so late how are you going to interpret me
to my dreams how are you that you are

Paraphernalia

I haven't put on
my ears this morning
however
the world is stunning me,
its multitude of chairs
tied together,
its stock market crashes,
that grinding of teeth
amid new shoes
and banknotes.

I think, with bullish insistence,
on what side of life
has life ended up?

The leopard skin
is trading on the market
at the price of a diamond.

Down the helter-skelter of fire
slide the passionate kisses
of lovers
falling into the spell of dark stars
with the cold days that wander
without a motherland
through tense cities
crammed with rubble.

No one whistles on the streets anymore.
And it seems embarrassing to long
for the calm blue sky
the yellow sound of wheat
the movement of water
in perfect circles
when a pebble

is thrown by a child
from the brightly-lit window of his room.

The pigeon returning
to the laid table
brings in its bloodied beak
a slap from the world.

How will I know from which direction
death will come.

The birth of the moon

> *And here lies the sea*
> *the sea where the stench of cities*
> *comes to shine like stars.*
>   Vicente Huidobro

The sky is black
and the shirts
hanging on a wire
are ruined in the discomfort
of funeral parlours.

In this unlikely morning
(half the sky
weeps buckets, in the other half
two suns sing like goldfinches)
I take a step
to recompose myself.

In my left pocket
a beaver weighs heavily
breathing, below my eyes
a clear morning

turns its back to the tar
gluing up the estuaries.

I put myself back together
gazing at the divided sea since my body
is in seven unequal parts.

The moon goes by nervously
smoking, down the corridors
of the ocean.

The asbestos cities
shine like wax candles
in the clenched hands of the dead.
And I'm hoping.

Everyday life

One would like to die
for each one of the dead
of this world
nevertheless it's never happened
that way

One runs to the nearest
chemist to salve
an everyday wound
or feels like savouring
his short holiday by the sea
while his nearest and dearest's heart
is shipwrecked
or on the fifth row
of the housing block
a small girl brings into the world
a thin root of light
or maybe rain

in quantities
never imagined before
not even
in the worst nightmares
of the flesh.

The working class don't go to paradise

The working class don't go to paradise—
they travel crammed into the entrails
of a thunderbolt or worse: inside the wing-blow
of a lightning flash, slender-bodied,
bold-faced, or topless.

The working class knit the sky's wounds
in the workshops of time
as well as on looms, dreaming,
depending on who reads this and where, depending on
who hears this, who understands it,
what might be their personal flag
or the homeland's flag, the north
of each individual, their entire life.

Depending on who's looking at it, how it's seen.
Here or in China the working class
do not go to paradise: they travel in torment
in the entrails of a lightning bolt crammed
inside the entrails of a chicken
struck dumb in the wingless breeze
which with a soundless blow
evaporates in the air
as a flash of lightning evaporates
in the heavy air of a storm
and vanishes
amid the old looms
of the sky.

Immortals

Those who at the request of darkness
go up to the platforms
and before the towers of heaven
justify their skimpy salary.

Those who, knowing in advance
that they will lose everything including their lives,
take charge of their discontent
and stand up,
walking down the streets
beating their chests,
covering billboards in the slogans of blood.

Those who despite fear
lack of faith
globalization
and uncertainty
go on believing in the heart's reasons
eternal love
and absolutes.

Those who blinded by
incomprehension's light
continue sowing daisies.

Those who were struck
by lightning and fire
and never cease
feeding doves.

Those who build plazas with hammocks
where people once rigged up bombs.

Those who shake away the dust
from abandoned tables
and lay out the tablecloth with 100 plates.

Those who wash the flags
(even though protocol says the opposite)

Those who shit on protocols.

Those who get married 17 times
so that love may be everlasting.

Those who hold out against the prod
the camp
the submarine
and returning to life
qualify as teachers
and build a school.

Those who
despite universal deafness
construct musical instruments.

Those who believe the sea
doubles as a handkerchief.

Those who believe it's possible
to paint stars on the distant sky.

Those who believe the sky
is not so distant
and sometimes, on extraordinary occasions,
can be touched by the hand.

Those who love too much
and instead of adopting
Vietnamese children
go out to the suburbs
to work with those who have no sky.

Those who build boats in the desert.

Those who paint birds
in jail.
Those who dream of flying
with the birds.
Those who dream.
Those whose heads
are filled with birds.
Those who keep birds
in their heads.

Those who consider wrinkles
on the skin as decorations.

Those who cry each time
an old man dies
because at that moment one more library
goes up in flames.

Those who forsake comfort
and a warm stove
and, in a full-on asthma attack,
walk off into the forest
to change everything.
To change everything.
To change it.

Child and leopard

If with a mere
snap of the fingers
I could prevent you from suffering . . .
Or with my shoulder
brush aside your obligatory quota of pain;
the iron clouds that are
destined for each of us,

whether you move this way or that,
will drench us in either case.

Neither can I teach you
what fear is, since sooner or later
you'll understand it yourself,
though maybe you'll manage
to endure it in some
less dramatic way
than did your parents
grandparents, and distant ancestors
whom you will never meet.

Maybe then you will discover
that you've got saved up for you
a real fistful of wrinkles
and premature grey hairs
that come like a factory stamp.

For now I watch you drawing
with the assurance of a pure artist
driven only by the dazzling
of a world you've just begun to know.

Outside the leopard goes by,
silent and hard as a diamond.

Meanwhile, my daughter,
I look after your wings
and pray that you don't miss anything,
especially air and likewise
your joy which I defend
at whatever price
though it cost me my own light.

This is the time
we are summoned to live.

Outside the room
the leopard goes by
and the square where the hammocks swing
is empty.

It's cold
and I watch you drawing
on the misted glass of your window:
a house with its chimney,
a flower,
a yellow bird crossing
(so you say)
the sky of your room.

And I can't teach you
what fear is or stop you
from suffering, my dearest one, even if I drag
the sky and its clouds
somewhere else,
even if I take in
your share of destined rain
with this body wasted by love and years.

All the same
I'll try with a snap of the fingers
and see if I succeed.

NOTES ON CONTRIBUTORS

KATE ASHTON lives in the north of Scotland. Her work has appeared in the Shearsman Gallery, at www.shearsman.com, but this is her first publication in the magazine.

PAUL BATCHELOR's first full collection *The Sinking Road* was published by Bloodaxe Books in 2008. In 2009 he won The Times Stephen Spender Prize for his version of a passage from Canto V of Dante's *Inferno*, and in the same year won the 2009 Edwin Morgan International Poetry Competition for his poem 'Comeuppance'. He has completed a PhD on the poetry of Barry MacSweeney.

JAMES BELL lives in Devon, and has been the co-host of Exeter's Uncut Poets reading series for several years. His collections *the just vanished place* (2008) and *fishing for beginners* (2010) have been published by Tall-Lighthouse in London.

JAMES BERGER is Senior Lecturer in American Studies at Yale, and author of *After the End: Representations of Post-Apocalypse*.

RICHARD BERENGARTEN lives in Cambridge. His selected works are available in five hardcover volumes from Salt Publishing.

PETER BOYLE lives in Sydney. He is the author of several collections, most recently *The Apocrypha of William O'Shaunessey* (Vagabond, Sydney, 2009). His translation of the selected poems of Eugenio Montejo was published by Salt in 2004. He is also co-author with M.T.C. Cronin of the 2008 Shearsman volume *How Does a Man Who is Dead Reinvent His Body?: the Belated Love Poems of Thean Morris Caelli*.

MARIANNE BURTON is working on a PhD at the University of London. Her pamphlet, *The Devil's Cut* (Smith's Knoll), was a Poetry Book Society Choice.

MARTYN CRUCEFIX has published five collections, most recently *An English Nazareth* (Enitharmon, 2004). His translation of Rilke's *Duino Elegies* was published by Enitharmon in 2006, shortlisted for the Corneliu M Popescu Prize for European Poetry Translation, and hailed as "unlikely to be bettered for very many years" (*Magma*). His new collection, *Hurt*, will appear in 2010.

CARRIE ETTER's first full-length collection, *The Tethers*, was published by Seren in 2009; a chapbook, *The Son*, was published the same year by Oystercatcher Press, and was a Poetry Book Society Pamphlet Choice. Her anthology of experimental writing by UK women poets, *Infinite Difference*, appeared from Shearsman in March 2010, and her second full-length collection, *Divining for Starters* is due from Shearsman in 2011.

JANICE FIXTER was born in Kent and has lived in South East London ever since. She has a BA in psychology from London University, an MA in Creative Writing, the Arts and Education and a D.Phil. in Creative Writing (poetry) from Sussex University. She has two collections from Tall-Lighthouse, *Walking the Hawk* and *A Kind of Slow Motion*.

KIT FRYATT was born in Tehran in 1978 and has lived in Ireland since 1999. She lectures in English at the Mater Dei Institute of Education, and co-edits *POST*, the poetry and poetics web-journal of the Irish Centre for Poetry Studies. She runs the Wurm im Apfel reading series—which she started with Dylan Harris, its associated festival, Wurmfest, and the seriously small poetry imprint, Wurm Press.

MÓNICA GOMERY lives in Philadelphia and is a recent graduate of the Creative Writing program at Goddard College, where she studied with Jill Magi, Jen Hofer, and Metta Sama. She co-edits and publishes *Never on Time Journal*, and hosts a monthly poetry salon accompanying the journal.

RALPH HAWKINS has two collections from Shearsman, *The MOON, The Chief Hairdresser (highlights)* and *Goodbye to Marzipan*, as well as several previous publications. He lives in Essex.

ZIBA KARBASSI was born in 1974 in Tabriz, Iran. She left Iran in 1989 and now lives between London and Paris. She has published five volumes of poetry in Persian, all outside Iran, and continues to write prolifically. An entire volume of her poetry is being translated into English by Stephen Watts. the two poems here have already appeared in a chapbook

GERTRUD KOLMAR (1894–1943) was a German Jewish poet, and a cousin of Walter Benjamin; she died in Auschwitz. Her birth name was Gertrud Käthe Chodziesner; the pseudonym derives from the town of Kolmar, the German name for Polish Chodzież, then part of Prussia.

PHILIP KUHN lives on Dartmoor. Shearsman published his book-length poem, *at maimonides table*, in 2009. He is working on a complete translation of Gertrud Kolmar's *Welten* with ruth von zimmermann.

RACHEL LEHRMAN is an expatriate American poet living in London. She recently gained a PhD from Roehampton University. Her work features in the recently-published Shearsman anthology *Infinite Difference*.

SWANTJE LICHTENSTEIN lives in Cologne, and since 2007 has been Professor for literature, creative writing and media studies at the University of Applied Studies in Düsseldorf. She has two collections, *figurenflecken oder: blinde verschickung* (Rimbaud Verlag, Aachen, 2006), and *Landen* (Lyrikedition 2000, Munich, 2009).

RACHEL MCCARTHY is a climate-change scientist, and is also the Poetry Society's representative for East Devon, and organiser of the Exeter Stanza, *ExCite*. She is also co-host of *Blah Blah Blah*, an arts magazine radio show on Phonic FM.

VALERIA MELCHIORETTO is Italian and was born in the German part of Switzerland. She moved to the UK in the early '90s and holds a degree in Modern Drama and an MA in Fine Art. Salt published her first collection, *The End of Limbo*, in 2007.

DOUGLAS MESSERLI, who lives in Los Angeles, is the editor of *Green Integer* and publisher of Green Integer books. He has numerous poetry collections to his name and, as Kier Peters, he has written a number of plays. In 2004 he was named *Officier de l'ordre des arts et des lettres* by the French Government.

JORGE PALMA, poet and storyteller, was born in 1961 in Montevideo, where he still lives. For many years he has worked for newspapers and radio stations, and has also run literary and creative writing workshops, both poetry and prose. His poetry collections are *Entre el viento y la sombra* (1989), *El olvido* (1990), *La vía láctea (poesía 1987–1995)* (2006), *Diarios del cielo* (2006), *Lugar de las utopías (poesía 2001–2006)* (2007).

KEVIN PERRYMAN lives in Bavaria and runs the small press, Babel Verlag. His own publications include *Still Life* (Bonnefant Press, Banholt, Netherlands, 2008). He translates both into and out of German.

NATHAN SHEPHERDSON was born in Brisbane, and now lives in the Glasshouse mountains in south-east Queensland. He has won the Josephine Ulrick Poetry Prize twice (2004, 2006), the 2005 Arts Queensland Thomas Shapcott Award, the 2006 Newcastle Poetry Prize and the 2006 Arts Queensland Val Vallis Award. His first book *Sweeping the Light Back into the Mirror* (University of Queensland Press, 2006) won the Mary Gilmore Award. His most recent books are *what marian drew never told me about light*, published in 2008 by Small Change Press, and *Apples with Human Skin*, published by UQP in 2009.

TUPA SNYDER currently lives in Bombay. Her first collection, *No Man's Land* was published by Shearsman in 2007.

CRAIG WATSON lives in Rhode Island. The poems here are drawn from his *Blue Orpheus* manuscript which will be published by Shearsman Books in due course. His previous ten collections include *Secret Histories* (Burning Deck, Providence, RI, 2007).

STEPHEN WATTS is a poet and freelance translator living in London. His most recent publication is *Mountain Language – Lingua di montagna*, which was published in English with an Italian translation by Cristina Viti.

TAMAR YOSELOFF is an American expatriate living in London, and is the author of three collections, most recently *Fetch* (Salt Publishing, Cambridge, 2007). Salt also published her Kettle's Yard anthology, *A Room to Live In,* in 2007.

RUTH VON ZIMMERMANN's three professional passions are music, dance and language. Having spent the first half of her life in Germany, she came to study music in Dartington, England. She toured extensively as a klezmer musician before meeting Tango, which changed her career to becoming a Tango teacher and events organiser. Her collaboration with philip kuhn on *Welten* rekindled her fascination with the intricacies of language. Together with her two daughters, ruth lives in a communal house in South Devon, where she likes to feel the earth and grow her own vegetables.

www.ingramcontent.com/pod-product-compliance
Lightning Source LLC
Chambersburg PA
CBHW030949090426
42737CB00007B/555